E

FROM

BABEL

By Rev. Jean-Paul Engler

EISBN-13: 978-1546619031

ISBN-10: 1546619038

Rev. Jean-Paul Engler
Jean-Paul Engler Ministries – FSCO
PO Box 423
New Market, TN 37820
www.FSCOministries.org

Printed in the United states of America

FOREWORD

Jean-Paul Engler has done it again! *Escape From Babel* is what I call a real victory for the body of Christ and quite an unmasking, unveiling, and eye-opener of what is really going on behind the scenes. Most people (and even most Christians) are so busy and their lives are so cluttered they seldom take time to really look deeply into the affairs of this life, let alone look at spiritual things. Much of the body of Christ (and unfortunately much of its leadership) pays little attention to the activity in the spirit world.

Everything on this earth is being adjusted by the spirit realm on a moment-to-moment basis. We witness two things going on very strong, even here in my country, the United States of America. Number one, there is an attack against our republic (our governing documents). A democracy runs by majority rule, whether the majority is right, wrong, legal, illegal, or in line with the governing documents. A republic runs by its established documents and laws. In the United States we live by the great Constitution of the United States and its Bill of Rights. The attack against it is coming more from within than without, though it is totally being influenced overall by the forerunners (the spirits of the antichrist).

I also see an attack on the body of Christ, but our Kingdom is being attacked from within, just like the Constitution is being attacked mostly by Americans and by very few of our outside enemies. The body of Christ is attacking our very documents in this great kingdom of God, the Holy Scriptures. I've been watching them become perverted, distorted, diluted, and literally set aside. Many Christians are being told to not even read parts of the Bible or trust the teachings of Jesus Christ! If this were coming from some antichrist people, I would write it off and say "consider the source," but because it's coming from within our own Christian ranks, I say we should very much pay attention.

What Jean-Paul Engler has done in this book is to expose how the antichrist demons work, how they influence the human race, how they use humans as pawns, and what the ultimate goal is to destroy everything that is rock-solid and built upon the Rock, Jesus Christ.

I love the pages where Jean-Paul shows us Babel's influence on the world and domination of world leaders and what it has done to the philosophy and the mindset of the average human. We cannot look back through the Old Testament and say it's only history. These things are targeted for the day we're living in, and we're watching them manifest right now. Many scholars believe the person of the antichrist is already born and being trained and equipped to take over one-third of the world and influence the entire world. Our Bible refers to these things over and again. What you and I are witnessing right now is exactly what Jean-Paul is revealing—the activities of the day, the preparation of the human race for the appearance of the antichrist, and the preparation the body of Christ that is slowly becoming more and more worldly, more and more carnal, and certainly more and more liberal in their definitions of the Scriptures and what we tolerate, even in our own lifestyles. Jean-Paul refers to this in chapter five, "Babel's Influence on the Church."

I pray this book will wake up everyone. In fact, my prayer is that everyone gets of copy of it and is able to read it and take it to the prayer closet. It is not too late for us to turn many of these things, and even if we can't turn these things completely, we certainly can postpone the ultimate end result—the spirit of Babel and the antichrist influencing even the body of Christ. The Bible constantly talks about a remnant who will make a stand now AND in the last days and that we will be in the total resistance. Even if our numbers are smaller, we will increase greatly in power and strength.

I hope you know what side of the cross you're on. In other words, are you on the side with those who say to leave Jesus alone, He's done no harm, He's come to spare us? Are you on the list of those who will go to Paradise? Or are you on the other side of the cross, accusing God of wrongdoing and considering Him to be merely one of us. It is a day of decision. That's what this great book does. It opens your eyes, and by the time you're finished reading it, it will cause you to make one of the most important decisions of your entire life. Are you going to take the mark of the beast, or are you going to keep the mark of Christ?

Job well done, Brother Engler. You know I love you, I believe in you, and I hold you in high esteem. Your work in Christ is great, as a missionary and as an author.

Doc Barclay

Mark T. Barclay

PREACHER OF RIGHTEOUSNESS

INTRODUCTION

The spirit of Babel was such a severe threat that the Lord God Himself had to come down to earth and put an end to the building of the tower. That project presumed to challenge Almighty God's plan for humanity and even His heavenly abode.

Similar to the influence of the spirit of antichrist which long precedes the coming on the scene of the actual Antichrist, the spirit of Babel has been with us for a very long time. While God successfully stopped the completion of Babel's contemptuous plan, the spirit behind it has continued to defy God and His people throughout history.

In this book, we will unmask what is truly behind today's progressive globalization movement. We will also attempt to discover the identity of those who are relentlessly pushing this agenda forward and what their ultimate goal really is.

Not only will we assess the impact that the spirit of Babel has had on humanity throughout history, but also at how it is affecting the Church of Jesus-Christ around the world today.

We already know that conventional weapons are useless against principalities and powers such as the Babel spirit. But that does not mean that we're defenseless or powerless against it. We have indeed been given mighty and effective weapons to fight against the wiles of the devil in these last days. (Ephesians 6:12)

In this book, we will look at scriptural answers not only on how to stay clear from the influence of this evil spirit ourselves but also how we've been commissioned by God to help others escape its lethal grip.

Finally, while this book is primarily addressed to Christians, it is also a wake-up call for those who have been indecisive about choosing Christ as their Lord and Savior. Contrary to what some are teaching today, there are really only two choices available to any of us: heaven or hell, life or death, Jesus or Satan! My prayer is that in some way, this book will help you make the right choice!

TABLE OF CONTENTS

CHAPTER 1

THE SPIRIT OF BABEL

It would be extremely naïve for us to believe that Babel can be confined to a specific geographical location or limited to the biblical narrative found in Genesis 10 and 11.

So the LORD scattered them abroad from there over the face of all the earth, and they ceased building the city.

Gen 11:8

Indeed, God put an end to the construction of the tower and of the city, but by no means was this the end of the spirit that inspired the project in the first place.

Though the tower was never completed, we know that the city eventually was. It is located in today's Iraq and has been known throughout history by the name of Babylon.

As with all spiritual entities, it is difficult to pinpoint exactly when the spirit of Babel began its negative influence on humanity. What we do know, is that once before, God had to intervene in the affairs of man because their wickedness had reached an unacceptable level.

Then the LORD saw that the wickedness of man was great in the earth, and that every intent of the thoughts of his heart was only evil continually. And the LORD was sorry that He had made man on the earth, and He was grieved in His heart. So the LORD said, "I will destroy man whom I have created from the face of the earth, man and beast, creeping thing and birds of the air, for I am sorry that I have made them."

Genesis 6:5-7

Noah found grace in the sight of God. He and his family survived the flood and lived on to replenish the earth. But it only took a couple of generations before the people of Babel contested God with evil once more.

Noah had three sons: Shem, Ham, and Japheth. Nimrod, the mighty hunter who initiated the building of the tower of Babel, was a descendant of the lineage of Ham. Ham famously distinguished himself, by unashamedly looking upon the nakedness of his father. Noah eventually cursed him and his descendants because of it.

While his two brothers took great care in protecting the modesty of their father, Ham had no problem in making his father's nakedness a public matter. We'll revisit this event, when we look at the modern expression of the spirit of Babel, the Babylonian spirit later in this book.

Cush, was one of the sons of Ham, who in turn begot Nimrod. The DNA of the "general contractor" of Babel can be traced back to Ham, the cursed son of Noah!

WHAT'S WRONG WITH BUILDING A TOWER?

There is of course nothing intrinsically wrong with constructing a large tower. Throughout history, different civilizations have built monumental structures without ever being challenged by God. Indeed, modern developers compete as to who will build the highest structure in the world. Why was the building of the tower of Babel considered to be insulting to God?

We find the answer to our question in the following verse:

And they said, "Come, let us build ourselves a city, and a tower whose top is in the heavens; let us make a name for ourselves, lest we be scattered abroad over the face of the whole earth."

Genesis 11:4

NIMROD'S PROBLEM

We should all learn a lesson from Nimrod's wrong behavior. Like I said before, God has nothing against men who build towers, churches or monuments. What He does object to is the fact that it glorifies the creature, rather than God.

who exchanged the truth of God for the lie, and worshiped and served the creature rather than the Creator,

Romans 1:24-25

The other issue is that Nimrod undertook this project of his own initiative. We remember that David had a sincere desire to build God a temple. But he immediately withdrew from the project when he was told that it would be his son Solomon that would be given the responsibility to build it. This brings us to a very important point: if God has not given us the authority to do something, we cannot expect Him to give us the anointing we need to accomplish it! We know from Romans 13:1 that all authority comes from God. Consequently, if we don't have God's authority, all there is to fall back on is physical power, military power or the power of influence and persuasion!

Unless the LORD builds the house,
They labor in vain who build it;

Psalm 127:1

We all come up with good ideas occasionally. But this doesn't mean they're necessarily God ideas! How many honorable ministry initiatives have failed, because God did not initiate them!

God's main objection to Nimrod's project, was his motivation for building the tower. This could not have been an ordinary tower. No, its top had to reach all the way up to heaven! The second reason for its building was that it was to greatly increase the power and elevate the status of those leading its construction. Third, it was to be a monument to commemorate the unity of purpose necessary to realize this project to the glory of man.

ONE LANGUAGE... ONE PURPOSE

Another characteristic the people of Babel have in common with today's globalists is their exemplary solidarity in purpose. Very much like some political groups today, they stood as one man and would not allow dissention of any kind within the group.

Indeed the people are one and they all have one language, and this is what they begin to do; now nothing that they propose to do will be withheld from them.

Genesis 11:6

Furthermore, we're told that they shared a common language. This probably meant that they communicated with each other in a single tongue or dialect. But I believe that it goes much further than that. Is it possible that they were so committed to the completion of their evil objective that even their means of communication needed to contribute to its realization?

BABEL, FIRST ATTEMPT AT GLOBALIZATION

It appears that his group of people, led by their ambitious leader, Nimrod, had already achieved a measure of success in uniting the world, even before they came to the region of Shinar.

Now the whole earth had one language and one speech.

Genesis 11:1

The Bible doesn't provide any details on how Nimrod was able to put together such a homogenous team of people.

When CSI agents conduct an investigation involving serial killings, they invariably look for patterns left behind by the murderer. The study of these patterns usually leads to the identification of the perpetrator.

The devil's "fingerprints" can be found all over the crime scene of Babel! Because his crude manipulative methods have continued to work so well on unsuspecting humanity, there's been no reason for him to change his tactics.

You can be sure that the so called "unity" of the people of Babel, did not come without a struggle. We may never know how much deception, seduction, manipulation and intimidation were involved in achieving it!

AN EVIL M.O.

The first "crime scene" we may want to investigate, is located in the Garden of Eden, at the beginning of humanity.

And he said to the woman, "Has God indeed said, 'You shall not eat of every tree of the garden'?"

Genesis 3:1

DECEPTION

In John 8:44, Jesus rightly identifies the devil as the father of lies. He is indeed the master of deception. We can name deception as number one on a chronological list of four approaches the enemy uses to put men and women in bondage.

God has said, 'You shall not eat it, nor shall you touch it, lest you die.'"

Genesis 3:3

In the above verse, Eve misquoted, or shall I say embellished what God had said.

The more naïve and least informed a person is, the easier it will be to deceive them. Fortunately, at this point of the process, it is still relatively easy for someone to escape.

SEDUCTION

If the subject does not realize that he or she is being deceived and does not react to it vigorously, stage 2 or seduction is initiated.

Capitalizing on Eve's ignorance of God's instructions, the devil moved on to the next weapon in his arsenal. We should never forget that the devil knows the word of God and he won't hesitate to use it against us. I encourage you, the reader, to study and meditate on the word of God more than ever before.

Those among us that only hear the word of God sporadically, are not only spiritually anemic, but are also vulnerable to the devil's seductive schemes.

Then the serpent said to the woman, "You will not surely die. For God knows that in the day you eat of it your eyes will be opened, and you will be like God, knowing good and evil."

Genesis 3:4-5

Seduction usually works on two levels simultaneously. On one hand, it tries to convince the subject that there will be no consequences to their action. Then, it seduces them by offering them personal enhancement, self glorification or carnal gratification. Not only did the devil use this weapon on Eve, but he even tempted Jesus with it. The verses below clearly illustrate this point:

"If You are the Son of God, throw Yourself down. For it is written: "He shall give His angels charge over you, and in their hands they shall bear you up, lest you dash your foot against a stone."

Matthew 4:6

If you needed any further proof that the devil knows the word of God, this should definitely convince you! Satan tries to seduce Jesus by saying that there won't be any adverse consequences for His tempting of God.

"All these things I will give You if You will fall down and worship me."

Matthew 4:9

How did Jesus succeed in defeating the devil? By using the word of God. If you and I want to defeat dominions and spiritual powers of darkness, we must know the word of God and become skilled at using it as the awesome two edged sword God intended it to be!

While someone may have been both deceived and seduced, there still remains a chance for that person to escape out of the devil's snare. The story of the prodigal son serves as a powerful example: He had been deceived into believing that life would be better away from his father's house. He had been seduced to engage in what the Bible calls "prodigal living", but he finally came to himself, repented and returned to his father's house.

Regardless of how people have become trapped by the enemy, our responsibility is to deliver them out of his hands, and not to figure out how they were caught. If I found my pet caught in a trap, my first concern would be to deliver her from the trap. Finding out how she was trapped would have to come later.

Let me share what an African man shared with me about the ancestral method used in his country to capture live monkeys. It goes something like this: the hunter first locates a suitable tree in an area where monkeys usually congregate. He carefully carves a hole of a specific size into that tree and places a nut or other bait inside the hole. Before long, a monkey will be attracted by the smell of the bait and be seduced to the point of reaching into the hole to seize the desired spoil. As he tries to remove his clenched fist from the opening, he realizes that it will not come out. At least not as long as he holds on to the nut. Most monkeys, thus trapped, refuse to release the bait and are eventually captured alive through this method. What I want you to see, is that we may find men and women that have been trapped by the enemy through homosexuality, drugs, riotous living, etc. However, if they're willing to let go, we should be prepared to help them in whatever way we can.

MANIPULATION

Once this phase of the process is initiated, it generally means that the first two have functioned successfully. It also means

that some form of indoctrination or brainwashing has already taken place. I believe that it is essential for us to correctly "diagnose" the extent of indoctrination the men and women we are to rescue have been subjected to. This is why developing the gift the Bible describes in 1Corinthians 12:10 as discerning of spirits, is so important. The Word of God encourages us to seek the best gifts. In this instance, I believe this means that we should ask for the spiritual gifts that will be most effective in setting the captives free.

In the early stages, manipulation is generally not overly aggressive. The reason for this is that the political group, cult or gang does not want to exert such pressure on the subject, that they might scare away their prey in the process.

At first, street gangs will put a new recruit through a low level initiation process. But as each successive phase is passed, the requirements drastically increase. Many gangs actually require the killing of a rival gang member to complete the initiation process. Once the dedication of the new recruit and his or her commitment have been observed, they're finally welcomed as legitimate members of the gang.

A former Los Angeles gang member shared his personal initiation experience with me. After submitting to the various tests to evaluate his dedication to the group, he was ultimately asked to kill someone as the final hurdle before becoming a bona fide member of the gang. Thank God, as he was waiting in his car, loaded gun in hand, for an opportunity to shoot an innocent stranger, his father whom he had not seen sober in years, knocked on the driver's side window and asked to talk with him! Whatever his father told him, caused him to abandon street gang life and brought him to give his life to Jesus. Today, Victor is a wonderful faithful Christian who is preparing to serve God in full time ministry!

Whether we're talking about a cult, a street gang, a sectarian religion or a radical activist group, identifying this evil progression is fairly easy, when observed from the outside. But for those who are entangled in it, things might not be so simple.

People who're struggling in search of their own identity, are the easiest to manipulate. The cult, extremist religious group, gang and radical political group, will capitalize on this weakness and provide the subject with a cause they can identify with.

We don't have to look very far to find this process at work in our own backyard. Most of the teachers in our public schools and universities are ultra-liberal in their ideology. They exploit both their position as authority figures as well as the immaturity of their students, to brainwash them daily in their classrooms.

Christian parents who are doing their best to train their children in the way that they should go (Proverbs 22:6), often have to compete against teachers who tell their kids to go in the exact opposite direction. This happens while their tax money is paying the very salaries of those they're competing against!

INTIMIDATION

Before looking at several graphic examples of this evil M.O at work, let us talk about the fourth and final phase of the enslavement process.

There inevitably comes a time when some of those who have been deceived, seduced and manipulated, come to the realization that they've been put in bondage and now want to free themselves from it.

Notice that I said "some". Unfortunately, there are many who don't have the will, desire or courage to escape the snare they find themselves in.

PARTAKING IN THE PROVERBIAL KOOL-AID

You might recall the horrific 1978 event at the Peoples Temple compound in Guyana, where a deranged cult leader named Jim Jones led 900 of his followers to commit suicide. How could this many people be deceived to the point of causing their own children to swallow a poisonous drink, before partaking of it themselves?

My theory is that they had been consuming the proverbial poisoned Kool-Aid, long before any lethal substance was added to it!

A CASE IN POINT

Just because the manipulative practices of a cult don't end up in the mass suicide of its members, doesn't mean they're any less destructive. One noticeable example is the Church of Scientology. Talk about deception! This worldwide cult actually calls itself a "church". While the word church or ecclesia in Greek, is not unique to Christianity, placing a cross on top of the organization's buildings is extremely deceptive!

Placing deceptive labels on things and giving trust inspiring names to projects, is common practice in the "Babylonian " world. For example, "Planned Parenthood" sounds much less threatening than "Baby Killing Operation", doesn't it? Even if it was granted a non-profit tax exemption, the Scientology organization is not a church and it definitely is not Christian!

We might be tempted to mock the men and women who have fallen prey to this multimillion dollar organization. But when you look at the number of lives that have been destroyed by this cult, you can't help but feel sorry for the thousands of men and women who have fallen into their hands, so be led to pray for them.

THE INITIAL APPROACH

The first thing you learn in merchandising and advertizing is to make the initial approach as appealing and non-confrontational as possible. If you watch the promotional clip for the so-called Scientology "Church", chances are that you will not see anything shocking or repulsive in the presentation.

Beginning with the décor of the lobby, to the welcoming smiles of the "congregation", everything is conducive to making the initial contact a positive and memorably pleasant experience.

They push the impersonation of a "church" to the point of offering regular "services", complete with weddings and baby dedications!

Anyone that falls for the initial deception is ushered into the next level. New recruits are offered courses on communication and enhanced practical living. While they call them self improvement classes, I call them deceptive indoctrination! I don't know whether these initial classes are free or not. What is certain however, is that it takes a minimum of $250.000 for anyone to complete all the levels Scientology has to offer!

Manipulation doesn't even to begin to describe the abuse and control the people are subjected to. Members are encouraged to sever all ties with non scientologist family members. Couples are kept from spending time together and pregnant women are pressured into having abortions. Internet access is forbidden, phone calls are monitored and mail to the outside is systematically opened, screened and returned to the writer if the content is judged inappropriate.

Those "fortunate" enough to live on the Scientology's Hemet compound in California, live under constant surveillance inside a fenced property.

Security on the compound called Gold Base is very extensive. A great number of regular in addition to CCTV cameras, motion sensors, and razor tipped fences as well as strategically placed sniper nests can be seen on the property.

If asked about the need for such high security, they'll answer that it's for the purpose of keeping the property safe from unwanted intrusions. Those that have been able to escape, however, will tell you that its primary purposes it to discourage those on the inside from escaping!

Fortunately, some have been able to do just that. But how many more are still trapped inside? We cannot ignore the multitudes that are held captive in these virtual prisons. The only thing capable of liberating these men and women from the bondage they've been subjected to, is the truth. You and I possess that truth and we need to proclaim it whenever we have the opportunity to do so.

And you shall know the truth, and the truth shall make you free."

John 8:32

CHAPTER 2

THE BABYLONIAN EMPIRE

The Babylonian Empire was a real kingdom, located in the ancient region of Mesopotamia, situated between the Tigris and Euphrates rivers in today's modern Iraq.

After God scattered them over the face of the earth, not much is heard from the people of Babel. But much like the reassembling of the liquefied Terminator in the movie bearing that name, whatever was terminated when God put an end to Babel's construction project, came back to life in the form of the Babylonian Empire.

THE BABEL LEGACY

In the early years of his reign, Nebuchadnezzar was clearly influenced by the spirit of Babel.

His desire to extend his rule to the entire world is very characteristic. As we shall see in the next chapter, this is the trademark of every leader that's been infected by this spirit.

Nebuchadnezzar king of Babylon came to Jerusalem and besieged it.

Daniel 1:1

Another common trait we find among Babel inspired leaders, is that they don't respect anything, no matter how sacred or historically significant!

Today's Islamic extremists don't hesitate to destroy entire cities that have been declared World heritage sites by UNESCO. Surprisingly, they recently bulldozed the ancient city of Nimrod, which is believed to be where the Tower of Babel was originally constructed!

Let's return to Nebuchadnezzar. Not only did he steal the articles from God's house in Jerusalem, but he defiled these articles by displaying them in the house of the false god he worshiped!

with some of the articles of the house of God, which he carried into the land of Shinar to the house of his god; and he brought the articles into the treasure house of his god.

Daniel 1:2

DEMANDING TOTAL ALLEGIANCE

During the height of his reign and while under the influence of the Babel spirit, Nebuchadnezzar had a large statue of himself erected in the province of Babylon.

Here's something else Babel inspired leaders have in common. No matter how corrupt or ruthless their reign, while still alive, they put in place some monument or memorial they can be remembered by. Remember the statue of Saddam Hussein being pulled down after the fall of Baghdad? Incidentally, the "monument" does not necessarily have to be a physical statue.

It can be anything that leader wants to be remembered by. i.e., a so-called legacy a former president wants to be remembered by.

When the deception of a Babel infected person or group becomes delusional to the point of believing that only they have all the answers, they won't hesitate to impose their will by whatever means available, including threats and manipulation.

It is interesting to note that today's "Babylonian" globalists pretend to champion tolerance. But when you look at it a little closer, you will find them to be extremely intolerant of anything they're not in full agreement with. When Henry Ford rolled out his first mass produced automobiles in 1908, he jokingly said that people could order the car in any color they wished... as long as it was black! Today's progressive liberals, parading as champions of freedom, promise to give everyone a chance to express what's on their mind... as long as it agrees with their narrative, of course!

The democratic election process in America, is the ultimate symbol of constitutional freedom. "Babylonian" globalists actively encourage people to exercise their right to vote and are great at promoting free speech during the political campaign. Unless of course free speech and the elections don't go their way!

Examples of this double standard are very common. But we don't have to look further than the protests against the election of the recent President to prove this point. Had the results of the election been different and a group of conservatives had taken to the streets to protest the outcome, can you imagine the outrage of the mainstream globalist media?

Nebuchadnezzar tolerated the Israelite captive's worship of the One he himself called "the God of gods". That is, until that allegiance conflicted with the unconditional submission he demanded from his subjects!

Then a herald cried aloud: "To you it is commanded, O peoples, nations, and languages, that at the time you hear the sound of the horn, flute, harp, lyre, and psaltery, in symphony with all kinds of music, you shall fall down and worship the gold image that King Nebuchadnezzar has set up; and whoever does not fall down and worship shall be cast immediately into the midst of a burning fiery furnace."

Daniel 3:4-6

Of course this image was more than a work of art that Nebuchadnezzar wanted the people to admire. This statue symbolized the authority of the king and it actually elevated Nebuchadnezzar to the status of a god!

So deceived was the king, that he totally forgot what he had said about the only true God that had given Daniel the interpretation of his dream!

Then King Nebuchadnezzar fell on his face, prostrate before Daniel, and commanded that they should present an offering and incense to him. The king answered Daniel, and said, "Truly your God is the God of gods, the Lord of kings, and a revealer of secrets, since you could reveal this secret."

Daniel 2:46

NEBUCHADNEZZAR's DREAM

Nebuchadnezzar was the most powerful king to ever rule over the Babylonian Empire.

One night, he had a dream that greatly disturbed him. There were two major problems with his dream. Not only did he not know its interpretation, but he couldn't even describe what his dream was about! Talk about a challenge for the magicians, astrologers and Chaldeans of his court!

After entreating his Hebrew companions Hananiah, Mishael, and Azariah to pray for him, Daniel returned to his house to seek his God.

After receiving the interpretation to the king's dream and thanking God for this revelation, Daniel went to Arioch, who brought him into the presence of Nebuchadnezzar.

Not taking credit for the interpretation, but rather giving glory to the Lord for revealing it to him, Daniel proceeded to describe the dream to the king.

"You, O king, were watching; and behold, a great image! This great image, whose splendor was excellent, stood before you; and its form was awesome. This image's head was of fine gold , its chest and arms of silver, its belly and thighs of bronze, its legs of iron, its feet partly of iron and partly of clay.

Daniel 2:31-33

WHAT DOES IT ALL MEAN?

Daniel gives a description of the statue king Nebuchadnezzar had seen in his dream. We're also told about the composition of the statue that is all but homogenous. He then explains that the statue's head made of gold is in fact a representation of king Nebuchadnezzar's reign over the Babylonian kingdom.

He further explains that the chest and arms of the statue were made of silver. This represented a kingdom that was to follow and that would be somewhat inferior to his.

We're told that the belly and thighs of the statue were made of bronze. This also represents a kingdom that would succeed Nebuchadnezzar's.

The legs made of iron represent a kingdom that is split or divided.

Finally, the feet of the statue were made of partly iron and partly clay.

Nebuchadnezzar's statue

If we study the statue in light of history, we will better understand its prophetic significance:

Under Nebuchadnezzar II, Babylon was the most powerful empire the world had ever known. Its influence extended over the entire known world of that time. The head made of gold, represents the power and glory of the ancient kingdom, that begun in 606 B.C.

The chest and arms of the statue made of silver represent the Media-Persian Empire that succeeded the Babylonian empire in 536 B.C.

The Greek empire that came to power in 330 B.C is represented by the bronze belly and thighs of the statue.

The two legs of the statue represent the famous Roman Empire, whose power was eventually split between Rome and Constantinople.

A HOUSE DIVIDED

The feet of the statue partly made of iron and clay, refer to the present day. Allow me to spend some more time explaining the symbolism of the statue's feet and their spiritual significance.

The feet which are partly strong and partly weak, perfectly describe the fragility of the present day European Union. In spite of all the unification efforts that have been made since the Treaty of Rome was signed by Germany, France, Belgium, the Netherlands, Luxembourg and Italy, the European community remains the most divided and disparate group of nations in the world. What was to be a trading zone to foster economic interdependency, is today crumbling under its own weight!

There is such an economical imbalance between the stronger nations and the weaker ones, that homogeneity appears to be an impossible dream!

When the Euro was adopted in 1999, it was to bring economic uniformity to the continent. What it is today, is a large scale redistribution of wealth program with Greece, Italy and Spain as the "welfare recipients" with Germany and other wealthier nations as the proverbial "cash cows"!

Along with Israel becoming a nation on May 14th, 1948, the creation of the European Union at the Maastricht Treaty of 1992, are the most significant events in modern history. While I am convinced that Israel will go on, I firmly believe that we will soon witness the unraveling of the European Union!

You watched while a stone was cut out without hands, which struck the image on its feet of iron and clay, and broke them in pieces. Then the iron, the clay, the bronze, the silver, and the gold were crushed together, and became like chaff from the summer threshing floors; the wind carried them away so that no trace of them was found. And the stone that struck the image became a great mountain and filled the whole earth.

Daniel 2:34-35

IF A STATUE COULD TALK...

Nebuchadnezzar's statue of course cannot speak. But it eloquently tells us the story of successive kingdoms that competed against God for the ruler ship of the world.

The most significant portion of Nebuchadnezzar's dream is the part that describes how the statue will eventually be destroyed. But most importantly, it marks the end of the spirit of Babel's influence on the world.

The stone that was cut out without hands, represents the One the Bible calls the chief cornerstone, the Rock that is Christ, the author and finisher of our faith!

'The stone which the builders rejected
Has become the chief cornerstone.

Matthew 21:42

It should be a comfort to every Christian to know that the spirit of Babel will eventually be destroyed. But before that happens, we shouldn't ignore its negative influence on humanity or stand idly by as it destroys the lives of men and women around us!

CHAPTER 3

BABEL'S INFLUENCE ON THE WORLD

If we look at history through the lens of Scripture and with the help of the Holy Spirit, we will discover several instances where the spirit of Babel was behind some of the most significant global events the world has witnessed.

Beginning with the successive "empires" represented in Nebuchadnezzar's statue, we know that the motivation of their leaders was world conquest. But let's look at several other power thirsty individuals that may not have had such lofty objectives, but were driven by their evil thirst for power:

Today's neo-Babylonians won't hesitate to eliminate anyone that stands in their way. I am convinced that those who savagely kill innocent policeman in our cities are possessed by the Babel spirit. On an even larger scale, I suspect that those who are rioting, destroying property and burning cars in the streets to oppose the newly elected President of the United States, are acting under the influence of the Babel spirit. So certain are they of the validity of their evil plans that they won't even consider that the majority of Americans did not vote for their fellow neo Babylonian globalist!

WILLIAM THE CONQUEROR

Initially named William the Bastard, became William the Conqueror after defeating the English at the Battle of Hastings.

He spoke no English when he ascended the throne of England. As a result of the Norman invasion, French became the language spoken in England's courts and completely transformed the English language. The fact that someone with such an obscure "resume" and questionable family background, not only would ascend to the throne of England, but was able to impose his own language (French) on the English court, makes us suspect that he had the help of some spiritual entity. His influence resulted in the permanent transformation of the English language into what it is today. Do you remember how vitally important the language issue was in the building of the tower of Babel?

William's conquests never reached beyond Wales and the northern regions of England, but he is credited for building the notorious Tower of London. Sound familiar?

NAPOLEON BONAPARTE

Much like William the Conqueror, no one could have predicted that the child born Napoleon Buonaparte on August 15, 1769 in Ajaccio, Corsica, was destined to become one of the most powerful emperors in human history! His family line was modest and at 5' 2"", he was remarkably short in stature.

Napoleon lead a number of successful military campaigns, with the ultimate goal of conquering the entire world. His historic victory at the battle of Austerlitz against Russia and Austria brought the end of what had been The Holy Roman Empire.

His influence was not limited to military might. He instituted the Napoleonic Code that influenced the legal systems of more than 70 nations around the world!

In an effort to unify the masses around him, he imposed the

Metric System, which became the standard for measuring length and weights across Europe. It is still used in most countries of Europe to this day.

JOSEPH STALIN

Joseph Stalin, was born Iosif Vissarionovich Dzhugasshvili, on December 18, 1879 in the small village of Gori. His father was a cobbler and his mother a washerwomen. Like the afore-mentioned characters, there was no indication that this man would have such an influence on the course of history.

Millions of his citizens died during his reign of terror. Under his leadership, the USSR became the second country in the world to develop the nuclear bomb. He is also known for launching "The Great Plan for the Transformation of Nature" !!! *(emphasis mine)* Stalin obviously wasn't satisfied with nature as the Lord had created it!

Had it not been for America and Great Britain as well as the military leadership of General Patton, Joseph Stalin might have been successful in his quest to rule the world.

Just like Nebuchadnezzar and others before him, Stalin was very much a narcissist. He had statues erected and cities named after himself during his reign.

ADOLF HITLER

Adolf Hitler was born in Austria in 1889. Leader of the Nationalsozialistishe Deutsche Arbeiterpartei (Nazi Party), he was the Chancellor of Germany from 1933 to 1945. He was one of the most ruthless dictators the world has ever known.

Beginning with the invasion of Poland in 1939, he began his conquest of Europe and started World War II. But his ultimate goal, was to conquer the entire world!

He was responsible for the racially motivated Holocaust that killed 5.5 million Jews whom he labeled "sub-humans". He was also credited with the killing of an estimated 19.3 million civilians and prisoners of war.

By 1933, Hitler had achieved full control of all branches of German government. He began to suppress every form of opposition still remaining. The Social Democratic Party, his strongest opponent, was banned and its assets seized. On May 1933, all trade unions were forced to dissolve, their leaders arrested and some of them sent to concentration camps.

 Hitler eventually formed The German Labor Front, in an attempt to unite all workers, administrators and company owners, under his rulership, calling it Volksgemeinschaft, which translates "People's Community".

This evil leader was obviously not the first man to be possessed with the Babel spirit. But how was he able to convince the entire nation of Germany in following him in his delusional quest to conquer the world?

Hitler and his wife Eva Braun apparently committed suicide and their bodies were incinerated. But the spirit of Babel did not die with them. Until it finds a willing host in the person of the Antichrist, it will continue to influence, manipulate and intimidate anyone too passive or too naïve to fight against it!

If you have an opportunity to talk to a progressive globalist, you might want to ask him the following question: "How do your

efforts of bringing every nation in the world under your care and control, differ from the imperialist ambitions of people like Hitler or Napoleon Bonaparte?"

They will probably answer that they have no intention of conquering the world and they will be sincere in their response. They only want to impose their ideology on the world and rule over the masses. Is their goal different than that of classic imperialists, probably! But it is definitely just as wicked! Just as communists like Lenin and Carl Marks believed that they knew what was best for the people of Russia and the world, neo Babylonian globalists are convinced that they hold the answer to every problem the world will ever face.

Because they deny the very existence of God and of course His sovereignty, they presume to take His place in ruling people. They take on the responsibility preserving nature and regulating the world's population growth through abortion. They discourage citizens from wanting to maintain a national identity, while pushing their progressive global agenda.

ANTICHRIST – THE ULTIMATE NEO BABYLONIAN

As we look at famous, or rather infamous individuals that became hosts to the Babel spirit, we have to consider the one that has not yet been revealed, but who's been prophesied to rule over most of humanity in the last days.

Let us look at Scripture and study the characteristics of his personality and determine whether he meets the qualifications of a neo-Babylonian:

His power shall be mighty, but not by his own power; He shall destroy fearfully, And shall prosper and thrive; He shall destroy the mighty, and also the holy people."Through his cunning He shall cause deceit to prosper under his rule; And he shall exalt himself in his heart. He shall destroy many in their prosperity. He shall even rise against the Prince of princes;

Dan 8:24-25

1. Acquiring power by any and all means necessary, is a common practice among Neo Babylonians.

"Then the king shall do according to his own will: he shall exalt and magnify himself above every god, shall speak blasphemies against the God of gods, and shall prosper till the wrath has been accomplished; for what has been determined shall be done. He shall regard neither the God of his fathers nor the desire of women, nor regard any god; for he shall exalt himself above them all. But in their place he shall honor a god of fortresses; and a god which his fathers did not know he shall honor with gold and silver, with precious stones and pleasant things. Thus he shall act against the strongest fortresses with a foreign god, which he shall acknowledge, and advance its glory; and he shall cause them to rule over many, and divide the land for gain.

Daniel 11:36-39

2. He shall do according to his own will. Since the Antichrist will *"not regard the God of his fathers"*, he will not submit to anyone, but will act selfishly to advance his agenda.

3. He shall exalt himself and magnify himself above every god. Very much like fellow- Neo Babylonians like Saddam Hussein and Nebuchanezzar before him, he will elevate himself to the status of a god.

4. He shall speak blasphemies against the God of gods.

5. He shall act against the strongest fortresses **with a foreign god, which he shall acknowledge**, and advance its glory; and he shall cause them to rule over many. At the risk of shocking some of you, I strongly believe that this "foreign god" is named Allah, the god of the Muslims, who will join forces with the Antichrist and will become the executioner for the Antichrist in the last days! (see chapter on "The Spirit of Islam" in one of my previous books: The Unholy Alliance).

6. **He shall divide the land for gain**.
   One former U.S. President, who shall remain nameless, should also appear on our list of notorious Neo-Babylonian personalities. I actually believe that he is to the Antichrist, what John the Baptist was to Jesus: a forerunner that prepares the way for the one to come! He too, tirelessly worked for eight years to divide the country for political gain, using one of the oldest and most effective tactics in the devil's arsenal: dividing to conquer.

JEZEBEL

It wouldn't be right to close this chapter without mentioning one of the most wicked Neo Babylonian that ever lived. So representative of this spirit was this woman, that her name really should have been Jeze-babel!

The first mention of this evil women and her deceptive influence can be found in the following passage of scripture:

he took as wife Jezebel the daughter of Ethbaal, king of the Sidonians; and he went and served Baal and worshiped him.

1 Kings 16:31-32

We're not told about the method Jezebel used to bring King Ahab to worship a foreign god, but you can be sure that seduction and manipulation were involved in the process.

Just because Jezebel happened to be the most notorious neo Babylonian in human history, doesn't mean that this spirit is exclusive to women. I have in fact encountered many men who were just as controlling and manipulative as she was.

A FRIENDLY ADVICE TO WOMEN

I want to pause for a moment, to exhort every Christian woman that happens to be reading this book. God has graced you with natural beauty and special qualities men only wish they possessed. Like everything else God gives us stewardship over, we must only use what we've been given to glorify Him and not allow the devil to use these assets for evil. (Ephesians 4:27)

I'm convinced that not one woman of God deliberately wants to be used by the enemy in any way. But it's been my experience that the spirit of Jezebel is very much at work in the Church.

You might think that you have no influence on your husband and that he pays absolutely no attention to anything you tell him. That may be the impression he gives you, but I can assure you that no matter how gruff and seemingly insensitive he appears, not only is he paying attention to your words, but more importantly to your body language. You've probably heard the saying: "happy wife, happy life!" Nothing is more disturbing to a husband than coming home to a wife that is giving you the "cold shoulder"!

Woman of God, you have incredible power! Use it only to glorify God and not, like jezebel, to manipulate your husband to the point of hindering him in his serving the Lord!

WHAT JEZEBEL WANTS, JEZEBEL GETS

Ahab coveted a parcel of land that belonged to a Jezreelite by the name of Naboth. It seems like the king was prepared to offer just about anything to acquire it. But because it was part of the inheritance he had received from his father, Naboth was not willing to part with it.

So disappointed was Ahab, that he went home and did what most depressed people do: he went to bed and pouted!

In comes Jezebel, who asks him what is the matter and why he wouldn't eat. When she discovers the reason for her husband's sadness, she immediately comes up with a "solution". This is very typical behavior among Neo-Babylonians. No matter how extreme or wicked the problem or even the resolution of the problem, the end always justifies the means!

Then Jezebel his wife said to him, "You now exercise authority over Israel! Arise, eat food, and let your heart be cheerful; I will give you the vineyard of Naboth the Jezreelite."

1 Kings 21:7

Essentially what she's saying is: "don't let an unimportant detail like Naboth's unwillingness to sell you his land, stand between you and your owning it!" This is what I'd call deception and seduction at the highest level! Not only does she encourage Ahab to abuse his royal power, but she commits to deliver the coveted parcel to him, regardless of what it might take to get it!

This practice is definitely not unique to Jezebel. Ancient and modern "Babylonians" don't hesitate to use extreme measures to achieve their desired goal. They don't allow ethics to stand in the way of achieving their objectives and they do not have any moral compass. To them, those qualities are deemed cumbersome and counter-productive. Globalists don't hesitate to break the very laws they accuse others for breaking.

A NEO BABYLONIAN CALLED HAMAN

After these things King Ahasuerus promoted Haman, the son of Hammedatha the Agagite, and advanced him and set his seat above all the princes who were with him. And all the king's servants who were within the king's gate bowed and paid homage to Haman, for so the king had commanded concerning him. But Mordecai would not bow or pay homage. Then the king's servants who were within the king's gate said to Mordecai, "Why do you transgress the king's command?" Now it happened, when they spoke to him daily and he would not listen to them, that they told it to Haman, to see whether Mordecai's words would stand; for Mordecai had told them that he was a Jew. When Haman saw that Mordecai did not bow or pay him homage, Haman was filled with wrath. But he disdained to lay hands on Mordecai alone, for they had told him of the people of Mordecai. Instead, Haman sought to destroy all the Jews who were throughout the whole kingdom of Ahasuerus — the people of Mordecai.

Esther 3:1-6

Here we find a man that had achieved great success in the kingdom and had been promoted to rule over all the princes under King Ahasuerus' authority.

But like most Neo-Babylonians, no measure of success, power or wealth ever seems to be enough! Mordecai's refusal to bow or pay homage to Haman, was enough to ruin an otherwise perfect situation.

While Haman had the necessary authority to punish Mordicai for not submitting, we're told that "he disdained to lay hands on Mordecai alone". As we look at the modus operandi common to Neo-Babylonians, this detail is very significant: whenever the opportunity to cause maximum damage to your opponents presents itself, fully exploit it to your advantage.

I believe that Herod, who felt threatened by the birth of Jesus, perfectly fits the profile of a neo-Babylonian: it wasn't enough for him to order the elimination of the One whom he perceived to be a threat to his reign, but he ordered the destruction of every male under two in the region surrounding Bethlehem!

Then Herod , when he saw that he was deceived by the wise men, was exceedingly angry; and he sent forth and put to death all the male children who were in Bethlehem and in all its districts, from two years old and under,

Matthew 2:16

NEO BABYLONIANS IN JESUS DAY

Of all the people groups Jesus interacted with, the religious sect of the Pharisees were His greatest adversaries. Because they were convinced that only they had a grasp on what was best for humanity, they immediately viewed Jesus as a threat.

They invested much time and effort into convincing the Jewish population that they were the only ones qualified to speak on God's behalf. Therefore, we see why it was totally unacceptable for them to allow Jesus to proclaim such things as "I am the way, the truth, the life"!

We find this prideful and arrogant attitude among today's progressive neo Babylonian liberals. They are so convinced they possess all the answers for humanity, that they

systematically refuse to even consider other alternatives, regardless of how beneficial those alternatives might be to society!

SUPREME HYPOCRISY

For comparison's sake, let's look at the practices of modern day neo Babylonians as they compare to the Pharisees of Jesus' day.

Whether in the entertainment industry or in the political realm, Neo Babylonians will exploit any and all opportunities to generate personal career enhancing news. Some don't hesitate to exaggerate and even make up charitable endeavors. Here's what Jesus had to say about the Pharisees who engaged in such obnoxious behavior:

Therefore, when you do a charitable deed, do not sound a trumpet before you as the hypocrites do in the synagogues and in the streets, that they may have glory from men.

Matthew 6:2

Another trait shared among Neo-Babylonians, is the exploitation of whatever information, whether true or false, that could potentially be used to weaken or destroy anyone they perceive as adversaries.

We don't have to look much further than the recent U.S. Presidential elections, to see how the liberal media and the so-called Washington establishment used every opportunity to catch the Conservative candidate off guard.

But Jesus perceived their wickedness, and said, "Why do you test Me, you hypocrites ?

Matthew 22:18-19

In this instance, the Pharisees fully expected Jesus to make a compromising statement against the Roman occupant. Had He not responded in the way He did, they would have immediately brought their case before Pilate and would have accused Jesus of conspiracy against Rome.

One of the reasons the Pharisees were so jealous of Jesus, is that He was able to gather great crowds around Him. But at the end of His ministry on earth, He had only eleven disciples and even they didn't seem very committed to Him at the time.

Woe to you, scribes and Pharisees, hypocrites ! For you travel land and sea to win one proselyte, and when he is won, you make him twice as much a son of hell as yourselves.

Matt 23:15

Gathering large numbers of people to further their agenda, seems to be one of Neo-Babylonian's favorite pastimes. No efforts are spared and no expense seems too great, if it succeeds in getting the masses to join the cause! The Pharisees were able to manipulate an entire crowd in order to influence Pilate to have Jesus killed. They succeeded in having the crowd ask for the liberation of a murderer, while they demanded the crucifixion of Our Lord!

"But woe to you, scribes and Pharisees , hypocrites! For you shut up the kingdom of heaven against men; for you neither go in yourselves, nor do you allow those who are entering to go in.

Matthew 23:13

Neo Babylonians are master obstructers. Just like the Pharisees prevented many from entering the kingdom of God, today's globalists are doing everything in their power to keep men and women from embracing a vision of the world other than their own.

Woe to you Pharisees! For you love the best seats in the synagogues and greetings in the marketplaces.

Luke 11:43

Neo-Babylonians are so convinced of their philosophical or spiritual superiority, that they fully expect to receive special consideration from others. This arrogant attitude can clearly be found among today's Washington D.C. elite. As it relates to the law of the land or the Constitution for example, Neo Babylonians don't feel that they should be subjected to such rules. This explains why someone who has clearly broken the law and should have been imprisoned for it, not only gets a pass, but receives the nomination of her party to run for the U.S. Presidency!

Before closing this chapter, I want to share my thoughts on how we can help those who don't believe like we believe and who might have a more liberal view of the world than we do.

We have a tendency to neatly put everybody into some "box" of our own making. Not only is this unfair, but it can also be extremely dangerous. I have named quite a few things that characterize neo Babylonians. However, I urge you not to jump to conclusions too quickly. The only sure way for you to determine whether someone is an accomplished Neo Babylonian or simply someone that's severely misguided, is by means of spiritual discernment.

You will notice that as much as Jesus used every opportunity to address the Pharisees during His three and one half years of ministry, it seems that there came a time when He would no longer respond to them. Could it be that He had finally just given up on them and decided that there was nothing He could possibly say or do to convince them?

These words of Jesus' to His disciples are very significant:

Let them alone. They are blind leaders of the blind.

Matthew 15:14

Clearly Jesus didn't want his disciples to waste any more unnecessary time or energy trying to convince some Pharisees He recognized to be irremediably lost. But that doesn't mean that we should arbitrarily cross people or people groups from our list of humans we witness to or try to rescue. We know of at least one Pharisee who believed and who risked his life by helping in giving Jesus a proper burial.

His name was Nicodemus. Although very timid and reluctant to openly express his belief in Jesus, the Messiah, I believe that in the final analysis, he became a genuine disciple of Our Lord.

Let's not forget that Paul, who was trained as a Pharisee under Gamaliel, went on to become one the greatest Apostles of Jesus-Christ!

CHAPTER 4

ONE WORLD... ONE LANGUAGE

The unifying factor of having one language was so powerful that the Lord Himself was sure that nothing could stop the people of Babel from achieving whatever goal was set before them!

Indeed the people are one and they all have one language, and this is what they begin to do; now nothing that they propose to do will be withheld from them.

Genesis 11:6-7

While Christians enthusiastically sing "We are one in the Spirit" in churches all around the world, unity is a reality that still eludes us. The church of Corinth to whom the verse below was addressed, had not achieved the degree of unity Paul desired for them to have. But can we honestly say that we're any closer to that goal today?

Now I plead with you, brethren, by the name of our Lord Jesus Christ, that you all speak the same thing, and that there be no divisions among you, but that you be perfectly joined together in the same mind and in the same judgment.

1 Corinthians 1:10

Should we ever achieve the degree of unity the folks of Babel enjoyed in working at their evil project, there's no doubt that we'll be able to accomplish whatever God has set before us to do for His glory!

The construction of the tower of Babel ceased, because God had to put an end to it. But the unity among those who carry the torch of globalism and desire ultimate control over the masses today, is absolutely frightening!

Because of my extensive travels, I get to talk to people of various cultures and political persuasions. But no matter what their native tongue may be, globalists all around the world speak the same "language".

POLITICAL CORRECTNESS

Starting in the mid 90s, there's been a deliberate attempt by globalists to control what can be said and how it should be said. They claim to do this for the sake of political correctness. But they're actually imposing a new language on America: one that better fits their ideology and that conforms to their vision of the world. The double standard in this area is pretty obvious. On one hand, free speech laws are enforced to protect some of the most outrageous declarations made by neo-globalist activists, politicians or journalists. However, these same laws don't seem to apply when anything derogatory is directed at groups they've decided to protect.

Referring to this movement, Stanford University's Matthew Gentzlow tells us: *"There was this innovation in using language very strategically and very deliberately."*

The Bible calls those who have exchanged the natural use of their bodies for what is against nature, homosexuals. But this

Term was deemed offensive by the liberal crowd, so they replaced it with "gay", which they consider to be more complimentary.

It is in the American political arena that vocabulary underwent its greatest transformation. Black citizens became African Americans. Illegal immigrants became undocumented aliens, while Islamic terrorists are now identified as common criminals.

Because the transformation of a language is a long term process, the changes may not be immediately noticeable. Because of liberty of speech in America, infractions may not be prosecuted. But imagine if a more totalitarian globalist government was put in place. You can be sure that conformity to a strict language code will be forcibly imposed.

LANGUAGE, A MEANS TO ASSIMILATION.

As an immigrant, I came to America speaking just enough English to be dangerous! I immediately realized. that learning the language had to be my first priority if I was to become a true citizen of this great country.

You might think that as a French-speaking man, I didn't have too many options… and you would probably be right! But I'm not so sure that encouraging entire groups of foreigners to speak only their native language, is really helping them. To be sure, it will only delay or make the assimilation process more difficult.

Teaching foreign children math, literature and history in their native language, makes absolutely no sense. Unless of course the goal is precisely to keep them from integrating American society.

Consider this: approx. 20% of the U.S. population speaks a

language other than English in their homes. There are a number of areas in this country, where you would be hard pressed to find anyone that speaks English! These are Arabic or Spanish speaking enclaves, that have little or no contact with the rest of the American population. Do you really think that these folks will ever fully integrate our society?

It is one thing for some wanting to preserve their cultural traditions and culinary recipes, but not speaking the language of the country they pretend they want to be a part of should not be an option..

Encouraging people to remain separate by virtue of language and allowing them to have their own interpretation of the law, only makes sense to deranged Neo Babylonian globalists!

Because ultra-liberal globalists consider national identity to be a hindrance to their master plan of a one world government, they will continue to push their agenda to the point of allowing Sharia law to be accepted in certain American cities, while others will refuse to enforce the law of the land. They will replace it with one that is "customized" and more favorable to a particular segment the population .i.e sanctuary cities.

Just in case you're wondering if what I'm saying is just another conspiracy theory, do some research on the city of London England, where Sharia law is already in effect in a number of its boroughs.

LANGUAGE USED AS A WEAPON

Just because the criminal use of the tongue does not require a gun permit, those that recognize it to be a powerful weapon, use it skillfully and quite deliberately.

Death and life are in the power of the tongue ,

Proverbs 18:21

The word of God is very clear concerning the destructive power that can come out of someone's mouth.

All we have to do is look at how much controversy and hatred is being generated by the neo-Babylonian propaganda machine of the American mainstream media. Whether in written form in newspapers, or through television and radio broadcasts, the brainwashing of the masses is a relentless endeavor.

I know what you're going to say: "only those that choose to believe the lies are reading these newspapers and listening to these media outlets". Thank God! We still have alternate sources of information here in America. But what if you lived in the Soviet Union or in Europe, where the masses have been subjected exclusively to the neo-Babylonian brainwashing for decades?

Joseph Goebels famously once declared: *"If you tell a lie big enough and keep repeating it, people will eventually come to believe it."*

I have first hand experience in this area and I can assure you that, at least in this instance, Goebels was absolutely right! Even when talking to Christians who grew up in a society that constantly lies to them, it is surprising to discover how successful the manipulation and deception has been!

As Christians, we should never deceive or manipulate people with our words. We are to speak the truth, with the understanding that it has the ability to make people free. If we keep our mouths shut because we're fearful or because we feel intimidated, we will allow multitudes to be kept in bondage by the devil. As Edmund Burke famously said: ***"All that is necessary for the triumph of evil is that good men do nothing."***

We may not like to hear this. But most of the evil laws that have been implemented in America, have come about because we Christians, did not say or do anything to prevent them from happening. Of course we should never use the vile language many liberal globalists use to advance their cause. But that doesn't mean that we should be quiet when our Christian values are being trampled on by politicians or the liberal media.

As I said before, we're at war against the powers of darkness that want to bring humanity into bondage. I believe the most effective ways to fight against it, is the spoken word of God.

I pray that God will raise men and women in our ranks, that can eloquently advance the cause of Christ in a way that will silence and shame our adversaries. May they be empowered by the wisdom and authority of the Lord!

THE STANDARD OF GOD'S WORD

Throughout this book, I've stressed how important language is, both to God and to humanity. From the unique language spoken by the builders of the Tower of Babel, to the morally and politically biased narrative of today's neo Babylonian globalists, it is essential that we pay attention to what people say about important issues. The Bible teaches us that what people say is an indication of what is really in their heart.

Brood of vipers! How can you, being evil, speak good things? For out of the abundance of the heart the mouth speaks.

Matthew 12:34

You might remember reading what I said about liberal globalists who speak the same "language" no matter what part of the world they live in. As Christians, we should also be speaking the same language, regardless of our ethnicity or cultural background.

Now I plead with you, brethren, by the name of our Lord Jesus Christ, that you all speak the same thing, and that there be no divisions among you, but that you be perfectly joined together in the same mind and in the same judgment.

1 Corinthians 1:10-11

As Christians, we're allowed to have different opinions on a variety of subjects. But if God's opinion on an issue is clearly expressed in His word, we are no longer entitled to our own. If we know God's opinion on a subject and express our opposition to it, we have effectively communicated that we are no longer Christians!

Why do you not understand My speech? Because you are not able to listen to My word. You are of your father the devil, and the desires of your father you want to do. He was a murderer from the beginning, and does not stand in the truth, because there is no truth in him. When he speaks a lie, he speaks from his own resources, for he is a liar and the father of it. But because I tell the truth, you do not believe Me. Which of you convicts Me of sin? And if I tell the truth, why do you not believe Me? He who is of God hears God's words; therefore you do not hear, because you are not of God."

John 8:43-47

The Pharisees proudly declared that they had Abraham and God as Fathers. But because they refused God's word, He identified them as children of the devil!

I am sorry if what I'm about to say offends any of my readers; but if someone who professes to be Christian tells me that they're in favor of fornication, homosexuality or illegal behavior, I will become extremely suspicious of their Christianity!

Every earthly language uses a dictionary to define the meaning of every word contained in that language. We Christians also have a dictionary. It is called the Bible! The word of God is the standard we must use to solve life problems, to evaluate every situation we face and discern whether the people we meet are really who they say they are.

For the word of God is living and powerful, and sharper than any two-edged sword, piercing even to the division of soul and spirit, and of joints and marrow, and is a discerner of the thoughts and intents of the heart. And there is no creature hidden from His sight, but all things are naked and open to the eyes of Him to whom we must give account.

Hebrews 4:12-13

In the text above, the word of God is correctly described as a weapon. But like every weapon, it is important that the one carrying it would have the skills to use it. Because the teaching of the word of God has been widely replaced by story- telling and motivational speeches in our pulpits, we're left with many unskilled Christians when it comes to its use.

For everyone who partakes only of milk is unskilled in the word of righteousness, for he is a babe. But solid food belongs to those who are of full age, that is, those who by reason of use have their senses exercised to discern both good and evil.

Hebrews 5:13

Do you remember my mention of the importance of discernment in one of the previous chapters? The knowledge and skillful use of the word of God will greatly help you in defending against evil in general and the spirit of Babel in particular.

SHIBBOLETH or SIBBOLET

Before closing this chapter, allow me to use a very unusual passage of Scripture to illustrate how important language is in relations between humans.

The Gileadites seized the fords of the Jordan before the Ephraimites arrived. And when any Ephraimite who escaped said, "Let me cross over," the men of Gilead would say to him, "Are you an Ephraimite?" If he said, "No," then they would say to him, "Then say,'Shibboleth'!" And he would say, "Sibboleth," for he could not pronounce it right. Then they would take him and kill him at the fords of the Jordan. There fell at that time forty-two thousand Ephraimites.

Judges 12:5-6

In this story, we find the people of Gilead identifying their enemies by making them pronounce a particular word.

I have found that a similar method can be used to determine whether we're dealing with a true child of God or a neo Babylonian globalist, pretending to be one.

In a previous chapter, I mentioned that liberal globalists speak the same language regardless of their country of origin or whatever their native tongue may be. Of course we shouldn't judge anyone based on their accent or on how successful they've been in mastering the English language. What I am suggesting here, is that we should at the very least know that the person in front of us is truly who he says he is. All we have to do is bring up words such as "abortion", "gay marriage", "illegal immigration" or "fornication" and then listen to what comes out of the person's mouth. Then we'll know with certainty whether the person is a Christian or a neo-Babylonian posing as one!

Neo Babylonian globalists are very serious when it comes to political correctness. They won't hesitate to initiate court proceedings against anyone who violates their language code by saying words considered to be offensive.

As Christians, we should at the very least have the right to find out who is on our side and who is clearly against us and the word of God.

I will never forget an incident I witnessed in a European church a few years ago. As I was ministering the word of the Lord to the congregation, I quoted Joshua's famous words: ***"But as for me and my house, we will serve the LORD."*** (Josh 24:15). I concluded by saying that if an unmarried son or daughter of mine ever decided to bring their companion to spend the night in their bedroom, I would not allow it under any circumstance.

To my surprise, the pastor's wife approached my spouse after the service. Apparently, my statement had highly offended her. Her own son had been sleeping with his girlfriend under her roof for over a year and she didn't see anything wrong with the situation. Her explanation was that "they loved each other very much"!

Call me old fashioned or judgmental, but I have a hard time believing that this person was a true Christian.

I look forward to the day when we will have the courage to call a cat a cat and like the Apostle Paul, won't hesitate to identify and separate ourselves from those who are only Christians by name or convenience.

But now I have written to you not to keep company with anyone named a brother, who is sexually immoral, or covetous, or an idolater, or a reviler, or a drunkard, or an extortioner — not even to eat with such a person.

1 Corinthians 5:11

PEACEFUL COEXISTENCE?

We already know what the ultimate fate of the Babylonian spirit will be. But the question is, how do we, as Christians, live our lives in an environment that is increasingly affected by its influence?

Thankfully, we're not the first group of people to be faced with this problem.

As previously stated, the spirit of Babel was very much in power in Egypt during the time of Israel's captivity. Much can be learned from the way God protected His people in the midst of such an adverse environment.

When the children of Israel first came to Egypt by Joseph's invitation, they were very much a part of Egyptian society. But once they became slaves to the Egyptians slaves, they refused to be absorbed and be a part of their culture. If we are to continue to live out our faith as the Church of Jesus Christ, we must never compromise our Christian identity.

And do not be conformed to this world,

Romans 12:1-2

Very much like the children of Israel must have felt before fleeing Egypt, we should realize that this world is not our permanent abode.

CHAPTER 5

BABEL's INFLUENCE ON THE CHURCH

We have just seen what an evil influence the spirit of Babel has had on the world throughout the ages.

One could only wish that the effects of the Babylonian system were limited to the world. Sadly enough, the spirit of Babel is very much at work in Christendom.

Like other demonic spirits, this spiritual entity will always seek the path of least resistance:

Be sober, be vigilant; because your adversary the devil walks about like a roaring lion, seeking whom he may devour. Resist him, steadfast in the faith,

I Peter 1:8-9

The Apostle Peter, who knew a thing or two about spiritual influences, encourages us to be vigilant and sober. We should never be so arrogant as to assume that we're so spiritually secure, that we cannot be affected by this evil spirit.

Therefore let him who thinks he stands take heed lest he fall.

1 Corinthians 10:12

THE FIGHT BETWEEN FLESH AND SPIRIT

The battle between the natural mind and the spirit has been raging ever since the fall of man in the Garden of Eden.

Because the carnal mind is enmity against God; for it is not subject to the law of God, nor indeed can be. So then, those who are in the flesh cannot please God.

Romans 8:7-8

The more a person is influenced by their carnal impulses, the more vulnerable they will be to the spirit of Babel.

Like the flow of water that always seeks the lowest possible point, the Babel spirit preys on those who are spiritually weak and emotionally vulnerable. Very much like a wild predator will identify and attack the weakest animal in the herd, the spirit of Babel will not waste its time pursuing strong Christians. Certainly not when there are so many easy targets available. This is why it's so important to remain spiritually fit, especially in these last days!

But you, beloved, building yourselves up on your most holy faith , praying in the Holy Spirit, keep yourselves in the love of God, looking for the mercy of our Lord Jesus Christ unto eternal life.

Jude 20-21

With an increasing number of churches actually catering to the carnal appetites of their members, the Body of Christ is faced with one of the greatest challenges in its history.

having a form of godliness but denying its power.

2 Timothy 3:5

The Roman Catholic Church initiated the Ecumenical Movement in the early 60's. The effort has only achieved limited success and has never really been able to unite Christian denominations in a significant way. Does that mean that the plans for a one world religion have been abandoned? Not at all!

Just like the idea of countries without borders could have scarcely be considered forty years ago, it is a reality today. Although in a limited form, it is known as the European Community.

The Ecumenical Movement may have failed in its attempt to create a global religion, but it's only a matter of time before we will witness this evil plan take shape. It used to be, that anything as obviously contrary to the will of God would immediately be rejected by the masses and particularly by Christians. But in a Church that has been indoctrinated by Oprah Winfrey and greatly deceived by an assortment of New Age gurus, there will be little or no resistance to the establishment of a one world religion

In recent years, we have seen the emergence of Chrislam, which is an attempt at merging Islam and Christianity. During Joint meetings, the Bible and the Quran are given equal attention Subjects that could potentially offend, are carefully avoided.

We can go on with our comfortable lives and ignore what is happening around us. But just because it doesn't affect us directly, doesn't mean it will go away! This is a very clear and present danger to the Church worldwide.

Every doctor will tell you that early detection and immediate treatment of cancer dramatically increase the chances of survival for a patient. The sooner we identify and take preventive action against these pernicious preachers, the healthier and stronger the Body of Christ will be.

And their message will spread like cancer

2 Timothy 2:17

Paul consecrated his life and ministry to the protection and preservation of the Church. Not only was he aware of the evil forces that were menacing the churches he was given oversight of, but he earnestly fought against them!

For I am jealous for you with godly jealousy. For I have betrothed you to one husband, that I may present you as a chaste virgin to Christ. But I fear, lest somehow, as the serpent deceived Eve by his craftiness, so your minds may be corrupted from the simplicity that is in Christ. For if he who comes preaches another Jesus whom we have not preached, or if you receive a different spirit which you have not received, or a different gospel which you have not accepted — you may well put up with it!

2 Corinthians 11:2-4

We are not responsible for what people do with the words of warning we give them. We are only responsible to God for delivering them. Whatever the outcome, at least their blood will not be on our hands!

If you're like me, confrontation is not something you look forward to. But that shouldn't keep us from obeying the word of God when it comes to rescuing those who have been lied to, mislead or manipulated by deceiving preachers

in humility correcting those who are in opposition, if God perhaps will grant them repentance, so that they may know the truth, and that they may come to their senses and escape the snare of the devil, having been taken captive by him to do his will.

2 Tim 2:25-26

INFECTED CHURCH LEADERS

We have seen the devastating effect evil leaders infected by the Babel spirit have had on the world throughout history. But think of the damage caused by those occupying positions of trust in the Christian community!

In the animal world, sheep are not particularly known for their discerning abilities or intelligence. Could that explain why so many of God's sheep are deceived by those the Bible calls hirelings, mercenaries and wolves? Some of the largest and fastest growing churches in America today, are lead by some I believe to be Neo-Babylonian "pastors"!

Beside not wanting to identify these imposters by name, there are simply too many of them in the Church today, that it would take an entire chapter just to list their names. But there is one that stands out as the poster child for the neo-Babylonian cause. In 1990, this famous activist was acquitted of felony charges for stealing $250.000 from his youth group. In 1993, he pleaded guilty to a misdemeanor, because he failed to file a state income tax return. In 2001, he spent 90 days in jail for trespassing charges. In 2005, he had to pay back $100.000 because he had exceeded federal limits on personal expenditures for his political campaign. This man is publicly encouraging his supporters to kill policeman. Let me ask you: looking at this man's resume with the understanding that he became an ordained minister at the age of 9, would you sit under his teaching? If your answer is yes, I have a parcel of swamp land I'm sure you'll be interested in buying!

THE TRADEMARK OF NEO BABYLONIANS

If any of us were asked to differentiate a mule from a zebra, we would immediately identify the zebra because of its characteristic stripes. One of the surest way to recognize a neo Babylonian, is that he doesn't hesitate to lie to achieve his objective.

Now the Spirit expressly says that in latter times some will depart from the faith, giving heed to deceiving spirits and doctrines of demons, speaking lies in hypocrisy,

1Timothy 4:1-2

Since the birth of the Church, there have always been false prophets, lying preachers and impostors in the ministry. Unfortunately, there will always be men and women that will fall for the latest fable. But there will soon be a time of reckoning for these ravenous wolves that are wreaking havoc in the Body of Christ!.

For offenses must come, but woe to that man by whom the offense comes!

Matthew 18:7

We must do everything in our power to warn and protect the vulnerable sheep in the flock. But we must also recognize when someone has reached such a level of rebellion, that the only thing left to do is let them go!

They went out from us, but they were not of us; for if they had been of us, they would have continued with us; but they went out that they might be made manifest, that none of them were of us.

1 John 2:19

WHAT ABOUT YOU?

While we're doing our best to be good Christians, in many ways, we are still very much human. As humans, we have a tendency to deflect attention away from us. But by doing so, we might erroneously assume that we are immune from the spirit of Babel.

Nothing could be further from the truth! The more we reject the possibility of "infection", the more vulnerable we are!

I have personally witnessed scores of Christian men and woman fall prey to the spirit of Babel. Sadly, they did so without being aware of the fact that they were being taken captive.

Whether his target is a Christian or a heathen, the devil's mission is to steal, kill and destroy. However, to reach his goal, his approach is quite different depending on who he is dealing with.

THE DEVIL, A MASTER BILLIARD PLAYER

The main difference between the game of pool and billiards is that you must use the table's cushions to hit the targeted ball in the latter. The devil understands that he cannot use a frontal approach when dealing with Christians.

Because Christians are armed and potentially dangerous to him, he uses an indirect mode of attack. His favorite and most effective "shot" against Christians, is the attraction of the flesh. In variable degrees, we still possess egos and still deal with emotions. The devil will of course use these weaknesses against us to his full advantage.

With more and more preachers willing to accommodate the carnal appetites of their audiences and catering to the egotistical ambitions of their listeners, we have an increasing number of Christians in danger of being infected by the spirit of the world and the spirit of Babel.

You might think that the "greasy grace" teachings and the "many ways to heaven "messages are just harmless passing fads. But they have already caused tremendous damage to the Church.

THE ANTIDOTE TO THE BABEL SPIRIT

Whether we realize it or not, we are faced with a spiritual epidemic of catastrophic proportions! When scientists deal with a natural epidemic, they implement measures to contain the spread of the disease and simultaneously isolate infected subjects from healthy populations.

These measures are just as valid in the spiritual realm as they are in the natural. But when it comes to fight a spiritual epidemic, that's where the analogy ends. Praise God, we are far better equipped than the scientific community.

For the word of God is living and powerful, and sharper than any two-edged sword , piercing even to the division of soul and spirit, and of joints and marrow, and is a discerner of the thoughts and intents of the heart.

Hebrews 4:12

Remember me saying that the devil knows that Christians are "armed and potentially dangerous" to him? Unfortunately, because many Christians are only served feel good stories, jokes and fables in church, they are not equipped with the most powerful weapon ever created: the word of God. And the small amount of the word they know, they don't have the skills to use it!

I will never forget the time when my wife Josette and a lady friend of hers, found themselves having to protect our home during my absence. As an intruder tried to brake in, both ladies

armed themselves with several weapons I had in the house. Unfortunately, neither one knew how to place the correct ammunition in the appropriate rifle. Thank God! The intruder eventually left our property without putting the two girls' marksmanship to the test!

If there ever was a time to perfect your understanding and the skillful use of the word of God, it is now! I urge you to sit under a pastor that actually teaches the word and study it as if your life depended on it. And it does!

Be diligent to present yourself approved to God, a worker who does not need to be ashamed, rightly dividing the word of truth.

2 Timothy 2:15

CHAPTER 6

ESCAPE FROM BABEL

As the world increasingly falls under the influence of the Babylonian spirit, what can we as Christians do to live in this kind of environment?

I know what you're thinking: let's pray that Jesus would take us out of this world and be done with it! I would agree with you, had Jesus not removed this option in one of His prayers:

I do not pray that You should take them out of the world, but that You should keep them from the evil one. They are not of the world, just as I am not of the world.

John 17:15-16

As much as we're instructed not to be of the world, we're assured of God's protection from the evil of this world. But we're also told that we will not be extracted from the world, until God's appointed time.

The quicker we realize that this world is no longer our God-ordained habitat, the more productive and fulfilling our lives on earth will be. Jesus never promised that life in this adverse environment would be easy. He only said that we could be over-comers of it by His power!

These things I have spoken to you, that in Me you may have peace. In the world you will have tribulation; but be of good cheer, I have overcome the world."

John 16:33

Yes! We can enjoy the kind of peace that passes all understanding, while the world around us is in turmoil and confusion! Yes! Not only can we thrive as Christians in this wicked environment, but we can be more than conquerors through Christ Jesus!

So how do we deal with the constant assaults made against our Christian faith? The first thing we have to understand, is that these attacks are not necessarily directed at us.

The first thing we have to understand, is that these attacks are not necessarily directed at us.

"If the world hates you, you know that it hated Me before it hated you. If you were of the world, the world would love its own. Yet because you are not of the world, but I chose you out of the world , therefore the world hates you.

John 15:20

Instead of reacting as if some strange thing was happening to us when we face adversity, we should rather be astonished when the world is conciliatory and understanding toward us. If the world accepts us, it could it be that we have so conformed to the world that we no longer stand out.

But evil men and impostors will grow worse and worse, deceiving and being deceived.

2 Timothy 3:13

We have been prophetically warned that things would get progressively worse, as our meeting with Jesus in the clouds approaches.

With variable success, the Jews obeyed God in keeping themselves separate from the influence of nations that worshiped other gods.

This includes the nations that were holding them captive. We already mentioned how the Israelites, even as slaves, kept themselves separate from the Egyptians. It is a matter of historical record that the Jews kept themselves from being absorbed by the nations they fled to during the Diaspora.

One of God's most powerful command for separation from the Babylonian spirit can be found in the book of Revelation:

And I heard another voice from heaven saying, "Come out of her, my people, lest you share her sins, and lest you receive of her plagues. For her sins have reached to heaven, and God has remembered her iniquities.

Revelation 18:4

As the Church of Jesus Christ, we're facing a very clear and present danger at this time. Christian men and women are under constant pressure from a world that is growing more evil with each passing day.

Christian adults are ridiculed by their co-workers and their children are marginalized by both teachers and classmates at school. All these are meant to force us into a mold of their choosing.

And do not be conformed to this world, but be transformed by the renewing of your mind, that you may prove what is that good and acceptable and perfect will of God.

Romans 12:2

This is much more than a political or philosophical issue. The spiritual implications are enormous! Not only must we resist the tremendous pressures the spirit of Babel exerts on us, but we must do everything we can to help our fellow believers escape the influence it has on them.

RENDERING TO CEASAR

As much as we are required to live on the earth in a holy manner and keep ourselves unspotted from the world (James 1:27), that doesn't mean that we can neglect our responsibilities as citizens or our duties as members of the society we live in.

We may want to live as hermits or retreat to a tranquil monastery to isolate ourselves from the evil that surrounds us. But how much influence would we then have on the men and women we are supposed to reach for Christ?

Those that are bent on evil, would like nothing more than for Christians to be silent and uninvolved. Does that mean that you should run for political office? Only you can answer that question. By all means, if God directs you to do so, I encourage you to seize every opportunity and go through every door the Lord opens for you. We need more "Esther's" and "Joseph's" that will walk in God's favor to execute the Lord's will on the earth in these last days.

Open your mouth for the speechless, in the cause of all who are appointed to die. Open your mouth, judge righteously, and plead the cause of the poor and needy.

Proverbs 31:8-9

One of the most embarrassing events involving God's people in the Bible, can be found in the book of 1 Samuel, when they were facing the Philistine army and their champion Goliath.

And the Philistine said, "I defy the armies of Israel this day; give me a man, that we may fight together." When Saul and all Israel heard these words of the Philistine, they were dismayed and greatly afraid.

1 Samuel 17:11

This is not the time for God's people to be dismayed or afraid! We need men and women with backbone that will use their God-given authority and wisdom to stand for what is right. Like

David, we should be outraged by what is being said and done against God and His children by His enemies.

Then David said to the Philistine, "You come to me with a sword, with a spear, and with a javelin. But I come to you in the name of the LORD of hosts, the God of the armies of Israel, whom you have defied.

1 Samuel 17:45-46

Whatever we do in fighting the Babylonian spirit, it must be by the Lord's command. No matter how fierce of an opponent we face, it will be no match for anointed Christians with fire in their bones and with a mandate from God!

Then he answered and spake unto me, saying, This is the word of the LORD unto Zerubbabel, saying, Not by might, nor by power, but by my spirit, saith the LORD of hosts.

Zechariah 4:6

CHAPTER 7

OVERCOMING THE SPIRIT OF BABEL

As previously stated in this book's introduction, we as Christians are not left defenseless against the Babel spirit. We have in fact been given spiritual authority to successfully fight against any spiritual force that would try to destroy the Church. Incidentally, the Church of Jesus-Christ is the only entity on earth that has been given a mandate from God to do so.

And I will give you the keys of the kingdom of heaven, and whatever you bind on earth will be bound in heaven, and whatever you loose on earth will be loosed in heaven."

Matthew 16:19

THE "ARSENIC" PRINCIPLE

We have all seen Hollywood movies, in which a spy is uncovered and has only one option: bite on the cyanide capsule concealed in his mouth, to avoid having to reveal important secrets under torture. The reason for choosing this type of poison is that its lethal effects are immediate.

Except for extreme circumstances such as the one described above, it would be very difficult to convince anyone to take this kind of poison voluntarily.

If the goal was to kill someone without them ever suspecting that you were trying to cause them harm, the poison of choice would be arsenic. Arsenic can easily be introduced in someone's food or drink without being detected. It will continue to accumulate in the victims system until it eventually kills them!

Because the Babylonian poison can enter someone's heart without them ever noticing it, Christians can be adversely affected and not even be aware of it! These are the people we are called to rescue

And on some have compassion, making a distinction; but others save with fear, pulling them out of the fire, hating even the garment defiled by the flesh.

Jude 22-23

In these verses, we are clearly instructed to consider three distinct approaches, depending on the people we're dealing with:

- *"On some have compassion"* I believe this refers to the multitude of unsaved men and women that find themselves in the "Valley of Decision" mentioned in Joel 3:14.

- *"making a distinction"* Here, we are instructed to use discernment when dealing with certain people with suspect motives and distorted belief systems. How many churches could have been spared if it's pastor had used discernment when a wolf in sheep's clothing came into the flock?

- **"save with fear, pulling them out of the fire, hating even the garment defiled by the flesh.** This has to do with those who have been so infected by the spirit of the world, by the flesh and the spirit of Babel. We are warned about the danger of being contaminated ourselves, if we're not careful, as we attempt to rescue them. As much as we might be willing to rescue those who are ready to be swallowed up by hell fire, I strongly discourage you from going on a mission to save people who're in this spiritual condition, unless you are spiritually strong and stable in your walk with the Lord. The devil would like nothing more than to use these people as bait, so he can pull you in to a place you really don't want to go!

THE TALE OF TWO MOUNTAINS

In the following pages, I will do my best to describe a revelation I have received from the Lord, concerning the very times we live in:

In a vision I saw two mountains of similar heights. Two armies were facing each other, but they remained on their respective hills. I was then taken to the passage of Scripture that relates the battle between the army of Israel and the Philistines.

The Philistines stood on a mountain on one side, and Israel stood on a mountain on the other side, with a valley between them.

1 Samuel 17:3

Before I continue with the vision, let me explain what was happening on this ancient battlefield:

A giant named Goliath would come out daily to challenge Saul's army. He was so powerful and fearsome, that Saul and his army were dismayed and greatly afraid as they listened to his threats. A single arrogant, but also confident man, defied the whole army of Israel! Granted, he was a giant... But, come on now, fighting an entire army singlehandedly?

In studying the characteristics of Babel infected people groups, I discovered the following common trait: they will not waste human resources unnecessarily, but will use the least amount of people to achieve the desired outcome. i.e. the Antichrist that becomes strong with a small number of people (Daniel 11:23)

I am often amazed at how few determined activists it takes, to change laws and practices that have long been a tradition in our nation. Because they are focused, relentless and united in their efforts, they're able to achieve incredible results, no matter how evil or misguided their objectives might be!

BATTLE LINES DEFINITLY DRAWN

I cannot fully explain what I'm about to say, but as I surveyed the mountainside on which the "enemy" was standing, I had the distinct impression that nothing could be done to change the minds, hearts or intentions of the people who had chosen to stand on that side. They stood in battle array as one man and it seemed as though nothing would be able to stop them.

As I looked at the other mountain in my vision, I saw those that represented the body of Christ in the present day. In stark contrast with the cohesiveness and disciplined attitude found on the other mountain, this group looked severely disorganized.

While some seemed focused and steadfast, others seemed to be too busy with their own affairs to be bothered by what was happening on the "other mountain" or anything else that didn't affect them directly. Thank God, I could also see a number of passionate, dedicated and on fire on this mountain.

THE VALLEY OF DECISION

In the passage above, we're only told of the existence of a valley between two mountains. But in my vision, I saw a very large expanse of land separating two mountains. Countless masses of people were huddled in this valley. They seemed confused, as they walked back and forth aimlessly.

The Lord then took me to the famous passage of scripture in Joel 3:14, that speaks to us about a spiritual valley.

Multitudes, multitudes in the valley of decision!
For the day of the LORD is near in the valley of decision.

Joel 3:14

Not only does this verse refer to the present time in human history, but it also tells us about the spiritual condition most of humanity would find itself in.

WHAT JUST HAPPENED?

As much as I want to refrain from talking about the social, political, spiritual and historical importance of what recently happened in America, I have to mention the following: a candidate that according to the media, the opposing party and even the pro-establishment members of his own party, did not have a chance to win the presidential election actually won, to everyone's surprise!

At the writing of this book, many are still in denial and refuse to accept what just happened. Riots are still going on in some of our major cities, while some political groups claim foul play and are making up all kinds of excuses for why they lost the election.

I personally rejoice over the outcome of this last presidential election. I can't imagine another four years of what I feel has been a deliberate attempt to weaken and destroy America. In a previous book titled "O America, Where Art Thou", I make the case of the previous President using his power to bring America down. Not satisfied with all the harm he has already brought on this nation, he has apparently formed a political organization whose mission will be to disrupt town hall meetings, organize riots and ultimately bring down the current administration! I must have missed something! But wasn't there a time where we made traitors to stand in front of a firing squad?

If you share my political views, you probably celebrated the outcome of the recent elections. But I want you to hear the word of warning I heard the Lord utter in the vision He gave me: "More than a victory, I want you to see this as an opportunity".

MULTITUDES ON THE MOUNTAIN OF INDECISION

What is the "Mountain of Indecision"? I know what you're thinking... This must be a misquote of Joel 3:14, but it's not. As much as the multitudes in the valley all seemed to be bewildered and confused, I also saw a surprisingly large number of supposedly Christian men and women, walking aimlessly to and fro, without focus or conviction.

Allow me to take you to one of the "mountain of decision" found in the bible.

So Ahab sent for all the children of Israel, and gathered the prophets together on Mount Carmel. And Elijah came to all the people, and said, "How long will you falter between two opinions? If the LORD is God, follow Him; but if Baal, follow him."

1 Kings 20:21

The mountain in question is Mount Carmel. Here we read that as Elijah was about to challenge the prophets of Baal, he first wanted to make sure the children of Israel were on God's side and not on the side of the enemy. He apparently must have discerned their spiritual indecisiveness.

As much as I look forward to the opportunity the Lord has given us to make His name glorious and reach the lost still in the "valley of decision", I also realize that we'll face some serious battles in the process. As much as Elijah needed to know who was truly with him on the mountain, we need to make sure that those who call themselves Christians are not going to turn against us, when the battle rages.

There are clearly many men and women who attend church today, that are "faltering between two opinions". While they pretend to be Christians, they consistently conform to the present world, rather than following the Word of God!

My thoughts are thus: if I ever found myself in a war situation and my life depended on the dedication and focus of the men and women alongside me in battle, I don't know about you, but, for example, it would be extremely difficult for me to trust someone that was confused about which bathroom he or she should be using. How can I trust such a person to distinguish between who his friends and who his enemies are?

CHOOSING WHOM WE WILL SERVE

There's yet another instance where God's people were challenged before going into battle:

In Joshua 24:14, we find that Joshua had already made up his mind as to whom he was going to serve. But before bringing all those who had survived the forty years in the wilderness into the Promised Land, he wanted to make absolutely sure that they weren't going to turn away from God, once they had crossed the Jordan.

"Now therefore, fear the LORD, serve Him in sincerity and in truth, and put away the gods which your fathers served on the other side of the River and in Egypt. Serve the LORD! And if it seems evil to you to serve the LORD, choose for yourselves this day whom you will serve, whether the gods which your fathers served that were on the other side of the River, or the gods of the Amorites, in whose land you dwell. But as for me and my house, we will serve the LORD."

Joshua 24:14-15

Right before Jesus had to face His greatest battle, one of the last things He did, was to unmask Judas Iscariot, the one "disciple" who had already decided to betray Him.

The outcome of the battle we're facing, is far too important for the Lord, the kingdom and the Church, for us to allow those we've identified as enemies of the faith, to fill our ranks. I know that in the current environment of political correctness, saying this sort of thing will not be pleasing to some, but then again, I'm not running for political office or a popularity contest.

It looks like the Apostle Paul didn't care much about what people would say about him identifying traitors in the ranks either:

"of whom are Hymenaeus and Alexander, whom I delivered to Satan that they may learn not to blaspheme ."

1 Timothy 1:20

LORD, PLEASE GIVE US DISCERNMENT!

As we are entering the period in history the Bible identifies as "perilous times" I find that wisdom and spiritual discernment seem to be in very short supply among God's people.

In a previous chapter, I mentioned the case of the Pharisees Jesus had to deal with for most of His earthly ministry. Because His discernment gift was so accurate, there came a time when He decided that He wouldn't waste any more time trying to convince them. He even asked His disciples to follow His lead. While we are never justified in condemning anyone, that should not keep us from exercising spiritual judgment.

And on some have compassion, making a distinction;   but others save with fear, pulling them out of the fire, hating even the garment defiled by the flesh.

Jude 22-23

Our Lord Jesus loves the entire world and gave His life for the salvation of all of humanity. We also, are to have compassion on all, whether friend or foe. We're in fact admonished to love our enemies!

I want to draw your attention to the second part of verse 22 above, where we're asked to make a distinction. Just because He loved everybody, Jesus did not deal with everyone unilaterally. As much as He extended His grace to the tax collectors and the prostitutes, He dealt very harshly with the Pharisees and Levites of His day.

Does that mean that He didn't love them? No. It just means that He didn't trust them and that He wasn't about to treat them as if they were His disciples!

Verse 23 refers to yet another distinct group of people. These are the ones God has called to rescue out of the fire of hell. After we've made our calling and election sure, we are to conduct "search and rescue" missions in what we already identified as "the valley of decision".

If we want our "mission" to succeed, there's one thing we must settle in our hearts and minds: everyone that we find in the "valley of decisions" is lost and in need of the Savior! Just because someone has had a religious experience, doesn't mean that they need Jesus any less than the ones who violently reject Him.

When Jude talks about those that we are to "save with fear, pulling them out of the fire", he is referring to those that urgently need to be rescued.

One of the most important military installations on a battlefield, is the Mobile Army Surgical Hospital unit. Because human lives are at stake, those responsible for triage, make the determination as to which wounded soldiers should be treated as a priority. Similarly, as we proceed through the "valley of decisions", spiritual discernment is of the utmost importance. It is not for us to determine who should be saved or not, but we need for the Holy Spirit to identify those that need immediate attention.

In the passage of Scripture below, we are given additional instructions on how to handle situations on the battlefield:

But avoid foolish disputes, genealogies, contentions, and strivings about the law; for they are unprofitable and useless. Reject a divisive man after the first and second admonition, knowing that such a person is warped and sinning, being self-condemned.

Titus 3:9-11

The first word I want us to pay attention to is *"avoid"*. We can waste an incredible amount of time and energy trying to convince someone to be saved with what we believe to be valid arguments. Mostly, all we're actually doing is frustrating and confusing the very person we're trying to enlighten!

What I found to be the most powerful way to bring someone to Christ, is to do what He did to reach the woman at the well: He listened to her and then gave her a word of knowledge by the Spirit of the Lord.

The second word is *"reject"*. I know, I know, this is not something that we want to hear in this politically correct environment we find ourselves in. But if we don't have the courage to confront those who are causing division among us, they will continue their destructive work unhindered.

Finally, I want us to look at the word *"knowing"*. Paul, who never hesitated to identify and reject those who were hurting the Church, also wanted the Thessalonians to know or recognize those among them who were edifying the Body of Christ.

And we urge you, brethren, to recognize those who labor among you, and are over you in the Lord and admonish you, and to esteem them very highly in love for their work's sake. Be at peace among yourselves.

1 Thessalonians 5:12-13

May the Lord grant us the spiritual discernment we need to know when to reject one and when to esteem another!

A HOLY SEPARATION

In most cases, separation is not something that is very much encouraged by the Word of God. There are however a number of instances where we're required to do just that:

"Come out from among them
And be separate , says the Lord."

2 Corinthians 6:17

While it's not always possible to separate ourselves geographically or socially from those we are asked to distance ourselves from, we're nevertheless required not to have communion with them.

Do not be unequally yoked together with unbelievers. For what fellowship has righteousness with lawlessness? And what communion has light with darkness? And what accord has Christ with Belial? Or what part has a believer with an unbeliever?

2 Corinthians 6:14-15

How can those of us having to work in a secular environment keep themselves from being influenced and contaminated by what is going on around them?

Allow me to share a testimony that might help those of you who find yourselves in this situation:

When I came to Christ in 1972, I was working in an automobile manufacturing plant in the Detroit area. Needless to say, that this was not the most spiritually conducive environment to be in. One of the most grievous things I had to endure, was the constant cussing and the taking of God's name in vain. Though I was a baby Christian at the time, I already knew that I had to find another way to deal with the problem than the method I used to resort to when I was a heathen. I remember offering a short and simple prayer to the Lord about the matter. Within only minutes, I felt as though an invisible dome had been placed over me. I could still hear the voices of the people around me, but it no longer affected me like it did before. The Lord did not immediately remove me from this environment, but He did effectively shield me from it's evil effects!

IS GOD A GLOBALIST?

If you view the events of Babel as I do, your answer will be no. However, should you need a little more information before making up your mind, allow me to explain.

More than the building of a tower and a city and forcing everyone to speak a single language, the Babelites were rebelling against God's design for nationhood. After the flood, God ordained a geographical, linguistic and ethnic separation between nations according to their bloodlines.

God designed nations to retain their distinctive characteristics. Does this mean that God forbade the interaction between one people group and another? Not at all! What God objects to, is the unrestrained influx of large numbers of foreigners into a society, to the point where that society risked losing its national identity.

I will make you a great nation;
I will bless you
And make your name great;
And you shall be a blessing.
I will bless those who bless you,

And I will curse him who curses you;
And in you all the families of the earth shall be blessed."

Genesis 12:2-3

These powerful words were of course addressed to the nation that bore the name of its patriarch, Israel. But this promise could very well apply to America as well.

I am not a proponent of what is called replacement theology. This false teaching implies that since Israel has failed to achieve the mission God had entrusted it with, the Christian Church was consequently chosen to accomplish it. Even more erroneous, is the idea that America has become God's replacement for Israel!

What I am saying is that America, like all nations for that matter, was chosen to fulfill a particular mission on the earth. While the purpose of some nations, like the United States, is to promote freedom and democracy, others believe they have a mandate to bring other countries under their control.

PEACE AT ALL COST?

In these particularly dangerous times, we cannot afford to misinterpret certain important Scriptures.

As we read John 10:10, John 14:27 and others, we can come away with the impression that Jesus only and exclusively brought peace to humanity. But if you balance these out with the passage below, we will have a much more accurate perspective on the subject of peace.

"Do not think that I came to bring peace on earth. I did not come to bring peace but a sword. For I have come to 'set a man against his father, a daughter against her mother, and a daughter-in-law against her mother-in-law'; and 'a man's enemies will be those of his own household.'

Matt 10:34-36

The word of God instructs us to be at peace to the best of our abilities and more importantly "as much as it depends on you"

If it is possible, as much as depends on you, live peaceably with all men.

Romans 12:18

Here, we are obviously offered some liberty in handling certain situations. This implies that it is not always possible to have peace, no matter how much you want to pursue it.

It also suggests that peace can only be achieved if both concerned parties agree to pursue it. The world considers "peace" to be an absence of open conflict. A physically abused woman might achieve what she believes to be relative peace by appeasing her violent husband, but all she has really achieved was submitting to bondage!

In the early days of World War II, Adolf Hitler approached the then President of France, General Petain, to offer him "peace". The General naively believed that he was getting a pass and France, like Switzerland, could remain neutral while the war raged across Europe. What Hitler actually obtained, was France's unconditional surrender in exchange for a small territory in central France with Vichy as a de facto capital.

For when they say, "Peace and safety!" then sudden destruction comes upon them,

1 Thessalonians 5:3

People say all kinds of things if they want to get something from you. Because Neo Babylonian globalists have absolutely no allegiance to America, they see no problem with allowing people crossing our borders, no matter what their intentions are. If a country isn't able to protect its borders, how can it preserve its sovereignty?

Call me intolerant or "deplorable' if you want, but I will not welcome anyone into my home unless I've made absolutely sure that their motives are pure. And once I allow them in and I find that they're in fact trying to run my home, I will kindly but firmly show them out! Wouldn't you? I won't apologize if people find anything wrong with that!

OPEN BORDERS AND IMMIGRATION

Our great nation is going through one of the most turbulent periods of its history. So much politically motivated propaganda has been pushed on our population by the liberal media, that you might be surprised by the responses you will get on the subject of open borders and immigration. Sometimes because of the personal relationship they have with an illegal immigrant or because they have been manipulated by politicians that exploited their naivety, people may favor open borders and unrestricted immigration.

But as Christians, it is important for us to know how God feels about these issues.

Now therefore, divide this land as an inheritance to the nine tribes and half the tribe of Manasseh."

Joshua 13:7

When God had Joshua assign each of the tribes of Israel a portion of the Promised land, He gave him strict orders about establishing borders between each territory.

There is a good reason why people put fences around their properties. The general purpose is to keep intruders out. I'm always amazed to find that the very same people who oppose border walls and fences, have no problem living in gated communities or behind the walls of their private properties! I have a suggestion for the people who favor open borders: leave the entry gate to your mansion wide open at night and be sure to keep your front door unlocked for a few days. We'll pick up our conversation on the subject after your house has been robbed and your wife and children have been threatened… or worse!

As an immigrant myself, I can certainly understand why people would want to come to America and start a new life in the "Land of opportunity". But shouldn't the host country be able to decide whom it should let in and whom it shouldn't?

If the mayor of a U.S. city is so concerned about the welfare of people who can't make a decent living in their native country. my suggestion is for him move to one of these poor countries and offer his services as mayor of one of the local communities. This would make so much more sense than making his municipality a sanctuary city and force unwanted populations on an already strained job market and overburdened welfare system.

As much as God encouraged the Israelites to treat strangers with fairness and respect, He also cautioned them to restrict the number of foreigners allowed in their land and to limit their influence on the rest of the population. In fact, He severely rebuked Solomon for marrying some of the foreign women he'd brought in to the land of Israel.

But King Solomon loved many foreign women, as well as the daughter of Pharaoh: women of the Moabites, Ammonites, Edomites , Sidonians, and Hittites — from the nations of whom the LORD had said to the children of Israel, "You shall not intermarry with them, nor they with you. Surely they will turn away your hearts after their gods.

1 Kings 11:1-2

Is it any wonder that our beloved country has become so spiritually confused in the last few years? What was once a Christian nation on whom God has poured out His grace, has become the land of "many ways to heaven" and "Chrislam".

So the LORD became angry with Solomon, because his heart had turned from the LORD God of Israel, who had appeared to him twice, and had commanded him concerning this thing, that he should not go after other gods; but he did not keep what the LORD had commended.

1 Kings 11:9-10

I am certainly not a proponent of ethical purity, nor am I against mixed marriages. What I am very much against, is the overwhelming introduction of millions of immigrants into our land with the motivation of altering the very fabric of what America represents!

WHAT WE SHOULDN'T DO

As much as we're taught not to endorse a person for ministry with precipitation, we also should be careful not to write people off prematurely. When the servants in one of Jesus' parables asked Him whether they should dispose of the tares the enemy had sown among the good wheat, He strongly warned them not to do so:

The servants said to him, 'Do you want us then to go and gather them up?' But he said, 'No, lest while you gather up the tares you also uproot the wheat with them. Let both grow together until the harvest, and at the time of harvest I will say to the reapers, "First gather together the tares and bind them in bundles to burn them, but gather the wheat into my barn."'

Matthew 13:28-30

If you're a Conservative, it would be very easy to condemn liberals for having convictions that are different from your own. As Republicans, we may be tempted to judge people just on the basis of being Democrats.

We are at war. But before we engage in the fight, we need to clearly define who we're fighting against. Our real enemy, the devil, would like nothing more than for us to be distracted by our political or social differences.

Immediately after being entrusted by God to take His people into the Promised land, Joshua was warned about not being distracted. The Lord knew that he would have to make very important decisions while fighting various enemies. For all intended purposes, Rahab was to be considered and treated as an enemy. The other thing working against her, is the fact that she was a harlot!

Had Joshua acted only on preconceptions, Rahab's fate would have been sealed. But because of his godly discernment, Rahab and her family were spared. As the mother of Boaz, she became a part of the lineage of Jesus of Nazareth!

WHAT CAN WE DO?

I believe that I have done my best to identify the spirit of Babel and the effects it has had on the world and on the Church. But I would be failing in my mission, if I didn't at least offer some possible solutions.

The first and most important thing you can do, if you're not yet born again, is to give your life to Christ. This will afford you the protection of the precious blood of Jesus and equip you with the Christian "shield of faith" with which you will be able to quench all the fiery darts of the wicked one. Eph 6:16.

If you find yourself on what I call the "mountain of indecision" and feel that you are wavering in your faith, I urge you to make a sincere decision for Christ. The Apostle James clearly tells us that if we're double minded we won't receive anything from the Lord! James 1:7-8. I don't know about you, but I want God to answer my prayers. Don't you?

The third thing we should do, is pray and get into the word of God like never before! We must be spiritually fit and equipped to fight the battles before us. I don't know of a better or quicker way to get in spiritual "shape" than praying in the Holy Spirit. Jude 20.

The last thing I urge you to do is ask the Lord for the gift of discernment. You will begin to see the men and women around you in a brand new light. The Lord will direct you and help you in rescuing some from the path of destruction they're on. The Lord will also instruct you to separate yourself from others, in order for you to escape their evil influence.

Finally, I encourage you to reach out to the multitudes in the valley of decision. If you aren't quite ready to do that, can I ask you to at least to pray and intercede for them?

CONCLUSION

I pray that this book has answered some of the questions you've had concerning the current state of affairs in our country.

Because we have a tendency to only focus on individual events, I've done my best to give you, the reader, a broader perspective on what is developing right in front of our eyes.

When we read an article in a magazine or listen to a news report on TV or the radio, we often react emotionally (and sometimes overreact) to what we read or hear. If we fail to understand the underlying plan or the motivation behind the things people or people groups are doing, we could get very frustrated and even angry. This will eventually lead us to war against flesh and blood, which is exactly what the word of God forbids us to do.

My purpose for writing this book was certainly not to incite you to hunt down liberal globalists in order to bash them. But if I've helped you in identifying them, then I have achieved one of my objectives. If something I wrote made you decide to escape the influence of the Babylonian spirit, then I have been very successful. But if I was able to recruit you into God's army for the purpose of rescuing the multitudes that need Jesus and are now groping in the "valley of decision", than all the prayers, study time and research that went into this book will have been well worth it!

ENDORSEMENTS

This is a now word for the Body of Christ. It will be a challenging word for some, but it will reveal the work of the anti Christ, globalist spirit and its work in the world and how it has influenced the church. Get ready, because you might have bought into the globalist spirit, unknowingly. This will let you know if you have. It is a must read!

Pastor Tim Cross
Senior Pastor of Living Word of Muskegon
Muskegon, MI

Pastor Jean Paul Engler's newest book, "Escape From Babel," offers great discernment to any Christian who reads it in these Last Days where deception is so rampant. Few people recognize the influence of the spirit of the world upon the affairs of men and the Church. Escape From Babel helps us connect the dots between the seen and unseen world. I am both delighted and grateful for the illumination, insight, and timeliness of the truths unveiled by my friend in this book.

John Rasicci
Senior Pastor of Word of His Grace Church
Cayuga Falls, OH

ACKNOLEDEGMENTS

I want to thank my Lord and savior Jesus-Christ for prompting me to write this book and for His help in formulating it, with the understanding that without Him, nothing of value can be accomplished.

I also want to offer my gratitude to Alisha Vaupel. Not only has she assumed the final editing of this book with great excellence, but the manner and attitude with which she's done it, is a powerful testimony to the glory of God.

I also want to thank my wife Josette for encouraging me during the entire process of writing this book and for her valuable input. As we would discuss various topics, she greatly helped me in clarifying potentially confusing issues by offering wise suggestions.

CREDITS

Nebuchadnezzar's Dream
http://jeffmorton.blogspot.com/2012/08/nebuchadnezzars-statue-and-religions.html

Edmond Burke quote:
http://www.quotationspage.com/quotes/Edmund_Burke/

From *The Alpha and the Omega* - Chapter Three
by Jim A. Cornwell, Copyright © 1995, all rights reserved

Matthew Gentzkow quote
MATTHEW GENTZKOW Stanford University • Department of Economics 579 Serra Mall •Stanford , CA 94305 650-721-8375 • gentzkow@stanford.edu

OTHER BOOKS

By Rev. Jean-Paul Engler

A NEW DAY FOR MISSIONS

A comprehensive booklet on modern missions, for both those who're preparing for missions work and those who are called to support it.

THE WINNING CHURCH

A book that describes where the church stands today compared to how Jesus expects to find her when He returns. It also provides abundant scriptural instructions on how to be more effective as a member of the Body and preparing the church for His imminent return.

GRACE ANATOMY

This book presents a balanced approach on the subject of grace and provides believers effective scriptural weapons to fight the negative effects of the hyper grace teachings.

FAITH THAT ACTUALLY WORKS

Deals with the Subject of faith in a practical, clear, fresh and uncomplicated way!

UNHOLY ALIANCE

In this book, Rev. Engler reveals the end-time strategy involving three evil spiritual entities that have entered into partnership for the purpose of destroying Israel, America and the Church of Jesus-Christ

O AMERICA WHERE ART THOU

This book explains how America became a progressive globalist society in such a short period of time. Seen through the eyes of an immigrant, it offers a unique perspective on the process that resulted in the current situation.

F.S.C.O. – PO Box 423- New Market, TN - 37820

47370760R00060

Made in the USA
Middletown, DE
10 June 2019